100 DAYS OF KINDNESS

Spreading Happiness, Joy, and Love with 100 Acts of Random Kindness

JACOB REIMER

Disclaimer

While all attempts have been made to verify the information provided in this publication, neither the author nor the publisher assumes any responsibility for errors, omissions, or contrary interpretations of the subject matter herein.

This book is for entertainment purposes only. The views expressed are those of the author alone, and should not be taken as expert instruction or commands. The reader is responsible for his or her own actions.

Adherence to all applicable laws and regulations, including international, federal, state, and local governing professional licensing, business practices, advertising, and all other aspects of doing business in the US, Canada, or any other jurisdiction is the sole responsibility of the purchaser or reader.

Neither the author nor the publisher assumes any responsibility or liability whatsoever on the behalf of the purchaser or reader of these materials.

Any perceived slight of any individual or organization is purely unintentional.

ISBN: 0-9939579-4-3
ISBN-13: 978-0-9939579-4-9

TABLE OF CONTENTS

INTRODUCTION

The pursuit of selflessness is truly a noble one. Truly something that should be, and needs to be, actively pursued! The only way to combat the evils and hardships that we all are exposed to is through selfless acts of kindness. Offering free, no strings attached love to our fellow man.

Truly, there is no greater good in this world, than doing good for the sake of others and not oneself.

By simply purchasing and reading this book, YOU have already taken the first step, and for that I commend you. However, I would also like to challenge you to not just "read" this book, but actually understand what I'm trying to accomplish through it.

The easiest way for you to do so is to try at least **one** of these Acts of Random Kindness for yourself. Whether it be one of the Free and "easy" ones, or whether it be one from the "Big Idea's" list! No act is small, and it is also the changing of the heart that matters.

So please, love, share, and spread kindness to all those around you. For, if we can all manage that, then surely this world will be a better place.

Thank you and good luck!

FREE (Easy)

Day 1 – Day 15

Day #1

Tweet/Facebook a Genuine Compliment to 3 People RIGHT NOW!

-

Action: Sign in to your favourite social media platform, and pick 3 people either at random, or better yet 3 people that you know could use some encouraging.

Then think of a genuine compliment and let them know through private message. End by saying that you are thinking of them.

This may seem like something very small, but it can literally change someone's day.

Imagine if you suddenly got a very genuine and sincere compliment right now from a friend. AND that they said they were thinking of you. If that doesn't brighten up your day, then you are either:

A: Made of stone.

Or

B: Getting thousands of compliments daily.

Most of us are not.

We all crave the same thing. Affection. A sense of purpose and belonging. So why not share such an important gift with others? Especially when it's FREE to give.

Try it out :)

Cost: Free

Day #2

Smile at Strangers

-

Action: This may seem like something that everyone should just "do" naturally.

I mean, how can you really call smiling an Act of Random Kindness?

Here's how:

By the reactions I get from people.

That's right. As soon as stop seeing strangers eyes brighten up with just a simple "Good morning", followed by a genuine smile, THAT is when I will stop calling it an AoRK.

In addition, you would be amazed how few people actually do it nowadays.

Instead, I often find strangers looking down. Or, "casually" pulling out their phones just as we are about to pass. Just to avoid eye contact.

We have become so unsocial as a society, and I hate to blame technology, but...

I mean, it's MY generation that's really struggling. My friends would rather text than talk, and would rather pluck eyebrows than make friends with a stranger in a

Starbucks or gym.

We need to change this.

And a good way to do so is by making eye contact and smiling to those around you.

Give it a try!

Cost: Free

Day #3

Go Out of Your Way to Let a Car Go/Turn When You Have the Right of Way

-

Action: This is honestly something I always try and do. As long as it makes sense (as in, doing it doesn't cause mass confusion and/or a dangerous situation).

However, if you are simply crossing a street that a car has been waiting forever to turn on. Then why not let them go first?

I mean, it will only take 5-10 seconds to them to go. While it would take 20-30 for you to go. Plus, sometimes they miss there opportunity to turn and will have to wait another couple minutes.

You can also choose to walk behind the car instead of in front. If they are pulling out of sub division onto a main road and you are walking on the sidewalk. Just signal that you will go behind and then do so.

I find that most drivers are extremely grateful for such a small gesture, which makes it completely worth it.

I know some of you are thinking this really isn't an AoRK.

Oh isn't it? I believe doing this does far more than simply “saving” the driver an extra minute or so. I think the true kindness is in the fact that you are going out of your way to think outside of yourself.

Choosing to think of the person in front of you, instead of yourself.

This is REALLY where the kindness comes in, and people will be genuinely touched by your selflessness.

Cost: Free

Day #4

Take a Minute to Direct Someone Who is Lost, Even Though You're Rushing

-

Action: It's really easy to quickly blow someone off who needs help. Especially if you don't know them, or are in a rush.

I will admit, I am very guilty of doing this.

This is something I definitely need to work on. And I will!

Because, again, by doing so, by taking time out of your own busy life to care for someone else, you are showing them that they MATTER! That they are worth your time.

Keeping this in mind makes it much easier to muster up a little bit of patience, and help your fellow man as I'm sure you would love to be helped!

Let's work on this together, ok?

Deal.

Cost: Free

Day #5

Offer Your Seat Up on a Crowded Bus or Train

-

Action: This one may seem like a great idea in principle, but when the opportunity actually presents itself it can be tough.

Especially if you have a long ride ahead.

However, this is a fantastic way to spread the love and show your kindness towards others.

Ideally you would want to offer your seat to someone who is pregnant, disabled, or elderly. Though, if none are present don't let that stop you!

If you are a man, give your seat up to a women. If you are a women, give your seat up to someone older than you. There really aren't any rules. So do whatever feels right!

Trust me, the soreness in your legs and low back is temporary, but your good gesture may have a lasting effect on your stranger.

Cost: Free

Day #6

Let Someone Into Your Lane

-

Action: Again, easy to say, hard to do.

I, for one, get very frustrated when I drive. I rarely ever want to let in others, especially if they are trying to "cheat" by coming in late.

However, here are two things I try to keep in mind—one, they are probably in a rush just like you. Two, it might have been an honest mistake, and they really need to get over.

Instead of making there day any tougher than it has to be, and potentially causing a scene, just bite the bullet and let them in.

Even better if you can do it with a smile and wave.

I actually love doing this to people who are already ticked off, because how can they be angry when someone goes out of their way to be nice to them. ;)

Just something to keep in mind next time you're driving in that icky traffic!

Cost: Free

Day #7

Let the Person Behind You At the Store Checkout Ahead of You If They Have Just One or Two Items

-

Action: I can honestly speak from experience that this really does have a big effect on the lucky shopper.

Having learned this one by having someone do it for me, I have since tried to pay it forward by doing it for as many people as I can!

It can really be a huge bummer when you are just there to buy one little thing, only to have someone empty the shelves in front of you.

The best part about this Act of Random Kindness, is that usually the person is already frustrated by the fact he or she has to wait for you, that when you say "You can go ahead if you like" they freeze.

They feel so bad now for thinking such horrible thoughts about it, that they might just learn a lesson about judging a person, or situation, by its cover!

Definitely something to give a try next time the opportunity presents itself.

Cost: Free

Day #8

Write Something Nice on That Person's Updates Who Posts on Facebook Constantly

-

Action: Why? Because they are probably lonely, and this is the only way they know to get attention.

Of course, we don't necessarily want to reward such behavior so that they think this is the best way to get attention. Though, a simple compliment and a "like" can go a long way.

I have to throw a flag on the play again for myself. I REALLY hate that social media loudmouth.

But I just have to remind myself. We all want attention, so why not give a little to those who may not be as privileged relationally as we might be.

You might be surprised as to what happens.

Cost: Free

Day #9

Listen Intently

-

Action: Simple, and to the point.

We often get far too caught up in our own little worlds, that we can sometimes forget to slow down and listen.

Just as we love it when others listen to us, it can be equally rewarding to not only return the favor, but to do so intently and with a purpose.

If the person wants advice, then don't be afraid to offer some. It they don't, then don't be afraid to just sit there quietly and let them get what they need to off their chest.

Listening is a dying breed, and those who can do so well are in high demand! Not only in friendships and relationships, but also in the world of business and jobs!

It is truly one of the best assets a person can offer, but like all things, it needs to be practiced.

So why not give it a try?

Cost: Free

Day #10

Give Your Friend a Hug, Touch Their Arm, or Pat Them on the Back. So Many of Us Are Starved for Human Touch!

-

Action: I realize that this will probably get two very different reactions.

People will probably either LOVE or HATE this idea.

I, for one, love it. I love touching, and being intimate. Hugging others, holding their hands, etc. It's my main Love Language, therefore it comes naturally for me. As I'm sure it does for many of you as well.

However, there is also the other end of the spectrum, my sister. She hates touching. She'd rather pluck her eyebrows with crazy glue than hug me for no reason (and don't get me started on kissing!). Which is totally fine. It's not her love language. She shows, and prefers to reciprocate, love in different ways.

But here's the problem...

We, as human beings, NEED human touch. Like actually need it. I can't quote directly because I can't remember where I read it, but studies show that children's brain development has a direct relationship to how much they are touched as loved as they are growing.

It's really crazy stuff!

So here's my point. Don't feel like you need to go around hugging and kissing every stranger in sight, that would be weird. But just be aware that we all starve for human touch, and that some may not experience it as much as they'd like.

Let's try to stop the desensitization of our generation, by simply being there, and showing love for our fellow man!

Can we do that? Good.

Cost: Free

Day #11

Say "Thank You!" to a Janitor

-

Action: It may sound simple, but honestly, for what they do, they deserve it!

I'd like to say I do this all the time, but sadly I don't. I definitely did it with the main janitor at my school growing up. Mainly because he was such an amazing man that we actually became great friends, but I'd like to make it a habit of doing it more often for strangers.

Now I realize that this is their job and that they make money for doing it, but just take a second to think about what life would be like without them?

Dirty walkways, garbage everywhere, vomit and who knows what else plastered in public places. They are the glue that keeps society running behind the scenes. And it is because of this that they usually go unnoticed.

So, let's together make a vow to try and make it a habit of saying an honest "thank you!" to our janitors whenever we see them.

It's the least we can do.

Cost: Free

Day #12

Help Someone Who's Struggling With Heavy Bags

-

Action: That's right, men. I'm calling you out!

You see that old lady struggling with her bags? Or how about that mother who's trying to deal with her kids while carrying enough groceries to feed an army?

You see them? Good. Now let's go help them!

I know it's not always convenient, but going out of the way rarely is! (otherwise it wouldn't be called "going out of your way").

But it's not only extremely nice and helpful, but sometimes can really save someone a lot of time and aggravation.

I'm not just calling out the men here, ladies you can do this too.

Especially if you are young and eager, then there is no reason why you can't help that elderly man or women with his or her groceries!

Let's restore the image of our generation, and show people that we care about more than just our smartphones and iPods (I am guilty as well).

We can do it!

Cost: Free

Day #13

Spend A Few Minutes on Free Rice

-

Action: While most of us in the developed world are fortunate to have food, shelter and even, perhaps an iPad (or whatever device you find yourself reading this on), the sad truth is that there are almost a billion people on the planet – close to 12% of the Earth's population – that go hungry each day. I understand that not everyone has significant time, money or other resources to help out with issues like this—despite our better lives, we still have stress, work and issues of our own to deal with on a daily basis!

Which is why Free Rice (freerice.com) is such a great program: You can make a difference in the fight against hunger without paying a single cent—plus, you might just improve your own vocabulary, grammar and other skills as you do it. The site offers visitors questions of varying challenge levels—starting off easy, getting harder as you get 'em right. For each correct answer, the UN World Food Program will donate 10 grains of rice to hungry people around the world.

By the way, this is made possible through corporate sponsors—so it costs you nothing, and you can learn something in the process of giving back.

Cost: Free

Day #14

Stand Up For the Underdog

-

Action: Almost everyone remembers the schoolyard bully picking on the smaller kids. Even if your school was a little kinder, there were still people that needed a pick me up—a little help to fend off those bigger.

This doesn't end once we hit adulthood, though—and underdogs, while championed by the media and in the movies, often find themselves ignored in the name of progress or the "harsh realities" of "real life."

But it doesn't have to be that way—and don't think of this as giving out a free handout. Underdogs aren't weaker or less capable; they've just been granted less opportunity by the luck of the draw. Some of us are luckier than others. But we can all be kind, and part of doing that is helping balance the tables of fortune by standing up for the little guy.

Perhaps it's a young teacher at your child's school who has a great idea for a project, but isn't getting the support from her coworkers due to her age.

Maybe it's helping a friend's campaign for local government by answering phones, sending emails and putting up posters.

Or it could just be offering to watch a single parent's kid with your own while they're at work.

Standing up doesn't necessarily mean being aggressive or outwardly bold; it is often just a matter of upholding our beliefs and values in little ways.

So give the underdog a chance, and rebalance the scales in their favor by sacrificing a little sweat and time!

Cost: Free

Day #15

Share (Even if You Don't Really Want To)

-

Action: We all learned about sharing in kindergarten (I think so, at least—it's been a little while). But that doesn't mean we all learned how to share. The difference is simple: one involves actual, you know, sharing. So take action and share something—maybe it's a book that your friend has wanted to borrow. Maybe it's that old camera you have lying around that a friend's artistic minded daughter could use.

It's easy to think in selfish terms, given how competitive society is. But this cost me money, you might say—or worse, I might never get it back (and if I do, it'll be in tatters)! Sharing, however, shows great trust and is a demonstration of friendship, kindness and respect that mere words can rarely convey. Remember, your friends and colleagues live in the same competitive world as you—and as such, they surely understand, despite our all being taught the concept long ago, how infrequent wholly unselfish acts are. So buck the trend, listen to your friends, and then see if there's anything sitting around the house that could benefit them more than you. You don't have to give it away forever—you just have to open up and share a little bit.

I believe in you (and remember, it's free)!

Cost: Free

FREE
(Medium)

Day 16 – Day 30

Day #16

Take Someone's Shift As the Car-Pool Parent

-

Action: I'm not a parent, nor can I currently drive more than one passenger at a time (darn you stupid BC driving rules!), so for the time being I'm going to have to sit this one out. But that doesn't mean you have to!

Carpooling is a fantastic way to save money, and save the planet. Yay for multi-tasking!

But honestly, I can see the look in my mother's eyes when someone randomly offers to pick her and my little brother up without asking. It truly impacts her in a deep way as it allows her peace of mind (since we only have one car and there usually someone using it).

You don't have to do this ALL the time, but every once and a while can make a huge impact.

Who knows, maybe they will randomly return the favor when you least expect it!

Try it out.

Cost: Free (or maybe a little change in gas if they are way out of the way)

Day #17

Email or Write an Old Teacher Who Made a Difference in Your Life

-

Action: When I first heard of my initial thought was "Why the heck haven't I done this already?!"

Don't get me wrong, I pretty much hated high school (I mean the school part). I loved my friends for the most part, and REALLY loved playing sports! However, I was rarely excited to get into the classroom.

That being said, there are two distinct teachers that come to mind that really went out of their way to make class fun, and really bring the subject to life!

Crazy enough, these teachers taught Physics and Math. I before you say that I was probably just good at those subjects (which I kind of was...), keep in mind that these weren't the ONLY Math and Physics teachers I've ever had. In fact, my two LEAST favourite teachers of all time were my previous two Math teachers. So it had nothing to do with how much I liked or disliked the course.

Putting my high school past aside, I really feel like it's worth taking the time to let these special figures in your life KNOW just how big of an impact they made on you.

I mean, if they can take the time to go above and

beyond in making learning FUN, or by just being there for YOU, then should we have the time to let the know how much that meant to us?

I don't know about you, but I'm about to email Mr. Penner, and Ms. McMan right now, and let them know that they did make a difference... even if it was only in me. Which, in my opinion, makes all they did completely worth it.

Cost: Free

Day #18

Put Sticky Notes with Positive Slogans on the Mirrors in Restrooms

-

Action: Women, I'm going to be relying on you for this one!

Not that men don't also need encouragement, but let's be honest... how many men are actually going to do this? I hope I am wrong, but this doesn't sound like something any of my guy friends would do.

Not only that, but women are also subjected to FAR more negativity in their day to day life than men.

Too fat, too skinny, wear this, don't wear that. It's easy to see where all these body image issues come from. It's not that the women are superficial, but the world keeps telling them they need to be... and then when they are the world tell them how awful they are being superficial! It's crazy.

So ladies, let's try to combat the negativity with POSTIVITY!

Simply write down some things you'd love to hear on a few sticky notes, then place them in strategic public places for women to find. I feel like mirrors in restrooms work the best. Because it's a little more “hidden” and “safe”. That way they have a better chance of really reading it, and taking the compliment to heart!

Please do this for me ladies! :)

(Men, you can totally do this do! And I'll be even more impressed if you end up doing it.)

Cost: Free

Day #19

Give Someone a Tissue Who's Crying in Public, and Offer to Talk About it (If They Want To)

-

Action: This may not come up very often, but if it does you now know what you should do.

Keep in mind that not everyone will want to talk about it, and some may even react negatively for you even trying to help. Just keep in mind that this is because they are hurting, and are directing their hurt onto you even though they don't mean too.

The stranger doesn't need to be crying either. If you simply notice someone sitting alone away from the crowd, go up and talk to them. It won't always work out perfectly, but you'll never know unless you try.

And even if it only works once in ten tries, wouldn't that make it worth it?

Plus, you don't even know how even the gesture may affect them subconsciously. Perhaps after you're long gone they really think about what you just tried to do, and maybe that will be enough to show that they MATTER!

I really wish someone did this for me during my struggle with depression. The main cause of the depression was from simple loneliness, and who knows what would have happened if someone had simply made the effort to talk to me. I may have said "no thanks", but then that would be on me, and not on the person trying to make a difference.

This takes a lot of courage, but also can have one of greatest impacts!

Take a chance, and see what happens.

Cost: Free

Day #20

Write Someone a Letter. Like a Real Letter. With Paper and Pens and Stuff. Then Mail It!

-

Action: I know right? Absolute lunacy!

But hold on, before you write me off as some kind of lunatic, just hear me out.

Though physically writing and mailing letters can take TEN times longer to do than email, think about how you feel when you get mail?

I know for me that whenever I get mail I freak out! And if it's ever from someone other than my grandma (or a bill... bleh!) then I'm utterly speechless.

Something I've never felt from getting an email.

In fact, I once received a hand written letter from this girl I liked when I was twelve. My family had moved to Thailand to do some mission work, and I was REALLY missing my friends from home.

Then randomly one day I get this package. It was from her and I could barely contain myself.

It contained some worthless trinkets, and do-dads, but also contained a hand written letter specifically for ME. And honestly... I still feel touched today. It was something I will never forget.

In fact, it actually meant so much to me that I kept the letter. I still have it... almost a decade later. It's the thought that really made it special for me, and I keep it as a reminder of the incredible feeling it brought me.

Now knowing that, don't you want to write more letters?

Why not write one to that boy or girl you've always liked but never really had the guts to talk too?

Even if nothing happens because of it, I guarantee they will be touched by the thought, and impressed by your courage!

Cost: Free (Or however even much it costs for you to get a hold of a stamp!)

Day #21

Compliment Someone in Front of Others

-

Action: Complimenting others is awesome, but try doing it in front of others.

It can be scary, or feel weird, but just imagine how awesome they must feel? Knowing that you aren't afraid to speak the truth about you no matter who is listening.

I would really encourage younger people to do this. Especially those in middle and high school.

Unfortunately I know from personal experience that people tend to bond over the gossiping and tearing down of others. It's really sad.

However, the good news is that most of the time is isn't because all these kids are bad at heart, but instead just insecure. They know they can get a laugh out of saying something mean, and then others join in to get the same acceptance and attention as the first. This also means that no one dare go against the group and start saying something nice. This could have horrible consequences!... or could it?

What if instead, you had the courage to stand up and start off by saying nice things about someone, either present or not, and see what happens.

I know that when I started doing this people would usually do what they always do. Repeat what they hear in order to fit in. However now instead of saying foul things, they are paying each other compliments.

It's kind of like using peer pressure for good rather than evil. ;) tricky, I know! Haha.

But seriously, give it a try. I'm not saying it will be easy, I'm saying it will be worth it!

And at the very least, I will be proud of you!

Cost: Free

Day #22

Write Your Partner a List of Things You Love About Them

-

Action: One day, sit down, take out your notepad, and just start writing. Anything and everything that comes to your mind about your partner that you like.

Don't have a partner? (like me) don't worry! Pick someone else who you love instead. Like your mom, dad, siblings, friends, whoever!

Just take the time to think about them and write out everything you love!

There are no rules about how long or short the list need be, only that it should come from the heart and not be shallow or made up. Really dig deep to let that person know what it is about them that you couldn't live without.

It could be as simple as their smile, or as complex as the way they whisper "I love you" into your ear.

Then, once you are done, give it to them. Let them read it and watch the joy come into their eyes as they do so.

This can be incredibly powerful and really take your relationship to the next level.

Plus, now that they know what you like about them,

they might just do them more often! (don't get any ideas!).

Give it a shot, maybe they'll return the favor.

Cost: Free

Day #23

Keep an Extra Umbrella at Work or School and Let Someone Borrow it on Their Way Home if There's a Sudden Downpour

-

Action: This one's actually pretty easy. Just bring an extra umbrella with you one day, and keep it in the office or in your locker at school. Then all you need to do is wait.

Once that rainy day hits, boom! There's your opportunity to make someone's day!

We've all there, stuck in the rain without any protection. Cotton shirt soaking up every raindrop. Sticking to you like cold syrup. It sucks!

So why not try to be prepared for those who may not be as smart as you. (Ok... maybe not the best way to look at it, but still.)

There is nothing against a nice kind gesture such as this, and really, what's the worst that could happen. They steal your umbrella? Wow! How would you ever recover from something so close to your heart!

All jokes aside, this is truly a genuine gift that will cause a much greater impact than you may expect.

Do it, bring that umbrella... and wait.

Cost: Free (Or two bucks for an umbrella if you don't have an extra)

Day #24

Hang a Sign on a Bulletin Board That Says "Take What You Need" With Tear-Off Tabs at the Bottom for Love, Hope, Faith, and Courage

-

Action: This is a very simple act of kindness that can make a surprising impact in the lives of others. We've all seen signs for lost dogs, babysitters and tutoring services on the corkboards at our schools, places of work or worship and so forth. Rarely, however, do these notices serve to inspire others. We often pass by these boards located in well-travelled hallways after a rough day—perhaps our girlfriend has broken up with us, we've lost a job, or made some sort of error in judgment. These moments can feel lonely, especially when it seems like everyone around the bulletin board is leading a normal, happy life—texting, talking, smiling and walking without a care in the world.

In these moments of silent struggle, it helps to know that we aren't alone, and that someone has experienced our sadness and self-doubt. And the motivational message conveys that we are in good company while also providing a pick me up for the rest of the day.

Sometimes, the easiest way to keep our faith or courage is just to be reminded that it exists by being able to reach out and touching it.

Cost: Free

Day #25

Randomly Clean the Kitchen for Your Partner, Roommate, or Mother

-

Action: For those of you who hate cleaning, this might sound more like torture, but I assure you that this act of kindness is both easier than it looks and highly appreciated by all. A clean kitchen is a morale booster for everyone in the house—it acts as a mental cleanser, revitalizing everyone's spirits. Yes, even those who seem at home amidst the mess will experience a boost!

Not to mention that taking out the trash, cleaning off those crusty plates and scrubbing down the stove's drip pans (and don't forget about the microwave—it probably looks like a high school science experiment) will make your entire residence smell fresh and clean, too.

So, even if you can't stand your roommate, or your mom drives you crazy, this is one kindness that will benefit you just as much as everyone else (although, really, all these acts benefit you as much or more than the other person, just in more mysterious ways).

Cost: Free

Day #26

Clean Someone's Windshield at a Gas Station

-

Action: Okay, so maybe you should ask before you do this—we all have experienced people cleaning our windshield and asking for a handout (or, maybe you haven't, if you don't live in a big city).

But here's a way to do this as an act of kindness, instead of as a nuisance: strike up a conversation with the other person as they're pumping gas. Smile. And offer to give them a helping hand after you're done washing your own windshield. Not everyone will want your help, of course, but it never hurts to ask—and some will be thrilled with your unexpected kindness and effort.

And they'll be able to see the road better, too, so you'll help out other people that you won't ever even see!

Cost: Free

Day #27

Throw Out a Friend or Stranger's Trash at Lunch (or During the Day)

-

Action: This one is simple—just offer to take the trash of a co-worker, friend or even total stranger away with your own once lunch is done. This even works for things like the community garbage. Have a roommate? Take his stuff out with yours, and save him a trip.

It also works with the dishes at the dinner table—ask others if they are finished, and clear their plates with your own. It doesn't take you extra time, but it shows that you're listening, watching and paying attention to them.

Plus, everyone hates taking out the garbage, so this act is extra kind, and it doesn't cost you even a lick of time!

Cost: Free

Day #28

Photograph Tourists and Give Them the Pictures (or offer to email the pictures to them digitally)

-

Action: This, like the windshield cleaning option, is one you should clear with the other person before you take action. You don't want to look like a stalker by snapping photos from afar without any prior explanation!

But, when it's obvious there is a couple or group together, and that someone will be missing from the shots, take it upon yourself to offer your services as a photographer. It doesn't take long, and most people are too shy to ask for your help—but they'll cherish the memory of having everyone's smiling face in the shot of their vacation for the ages.

If they don't have a camera, and you have a camera of your own handy, offer to snap a picture and then email them the shots. This will be extra appreciated, as they might otherwise have nothing but a few gifts from the souvenir shop to remember their vacation by.

Cost: Free

Day #29

Already Sweeping Leaves or Shoveling the Snow Off Your Sidewalk? Do Your Neighbor's Sidewalk as Well!

-

Action: No one loves shoveling snow or sweeping leaves, so this idea might make your bones ache just thinking about it. But the extra hard work and grit will definitely go noticed by your neighbor. They'll appreciate your hard work and initiative, especially given the tough nature of the job. Plus, it helps clean up the neighborhood and keep your sidewalk looking clean, tidy and safe.

And, in the future, they'll remember this favor, and pay it forward—maybe you'll be down with the flu in the dead of winter, and there's a snowstorm. This time, they'll come to the rescue.

But don't do it because you expect anything in return; perform this kindness because, for the time investment, it's one of the best ways to pay it forward and show that you care about your community, neighbors and everyone around you.

Cost: Free

Day #30

Don't Leave Others Waiting for You

-

BE ON TIME!

Action: This is a simple kindness that many no doubt find difficult. Look, I get it—modern life is busy and commitments get in the way. You have appointments, classes, sports to watch (okay, maybe that last one can slide a little). But the point is, in a hectic world, it's tough to be on time.

Which makes being on time all the more important, kind and noteworthy—because you'll be one of the only people that does it! If others can rely on you, not only will they respect you and reciprocate in kind, you will greatly ease the stress and burden of their own lives. If you can be a positive in the lives of others—instead of a question mark and added source of anxiety—this is one of the greatest kindnesses you can give.

It doesn't cost a thing besides a little self-discipline (and maybe a little sleep, if you're a snoozer). But it pays huge benefits for those around you. Be someone others can rely on! They'll love you for it because you make their lives easier.

Cost: Free

FREE (Hard)

Day 31 – Day 45

Day #31

Round Up All the Shopping Carts Outside of a WalMart, Target, or Costco

-

Action: Okay, so maybe you're thinking that these places employ people to do this. That's true– but these folks have other duties, and they also have pretty tough jobs for not-so-great pay. Would you want to be yelled at by an over-zealous customer because a coupon didn't scan?

So give these hardworking people a hand and, at the very least, put your own cart in the designated rack outside the store. If you're feeling ambitious, round up the carts in the nearby area—people have a tendency to leave them just outside the chute where they're supposed to go.

And if you want to go the extra mile, snag all the stragglers sitting in parking spaces, on the sidewalk and in the planter boxes and return them to their rightful place.

The employees will thank you, even if they don't see you do it.

The other customers will also be appreciative, because they'll be able to find a cart (and they won't hit one with their car because one was left where it didn't belong).

Cost: Free

Day #32

Go out of your way to praise an employee who does great work to his boss personally

-

Action: You can do this act of kindness either face-to-face, by phone, or through email. Praise is appreciated in all its forms—particularly when it's a surprise!

I know, I know—in this world, it's easy to see your co-workers as competition instead of teammates. Even if you consider the people you work with friends, things can get testy when there's a promotion or bonus on the line.

Buck that trend and tendency instead, and actively talk up your co-workers to their boss. In team meetings, highlight other people's great ideas. Don't take all the credit for yourself—spread it around, even if an idea was your own. Try to showcase your co-worker's strengths and accomplishments.

Of course, don't give credit if none is due (it's not kind to lie to their boss). But if someone has contributed positively to a project, report or other important office function, let everyone know—especially the man in charge of making decisions. Their boss is busy, and she might not have the time to find out where all the good ideas are coming from.

So tell her, and help her and your fellow employee out in the process!

Cost: Free

Day #33

Go out of your way to spend time and befriend someone who is shy at school, work, or a get together.

-

Action: You don't have to marry the person, but just being nice. Introducing them to a few people can make a MASSIVE difference in their life.

Introverts often have a difficult time making friends. This is a shame, as they also often have lots of great skills and things to offer to those around them—they just don't advertise it and shout it from the rooftops. That can mean that we think of shy and quiet people as "weird" or "outcasts," but it really just means that maybe we haven't made enough of an effort to learn who they really are.

So make that effort—ask them about themselves, include them in the conversation, and invite them out for drinks or lunch. Get to know their passions and what makes them tick. They're probably thinking a lot, since they don't speak as much—so give them a chance to share their ideas and thoughts with the world!

They'll benefit, and you'll probably benefit more than you can imagine, too.

Cost: Free

Day #34

Become a Big Brother or Big Sister

-

Action: Big Brothers Big Sisters (bbbs.org) is a one-on-one mentoring program that pairs a role model (that's you) with a kid. But think of it more like a friendship—just that you're a little older, a little wiser, and can help the kid reach his fullest potential by steering him away from all the pitfalls that life presents us with.

The organization screens its applicants pretty heavily, so you must have a clean record and meet other criterion to be eligible. But this process also allows them to match you with a child that meets your own interests, strengths and personality.

This one can be pretty tough, and takes a lot of time to do right. Giving kids advice and showing them the ropes of living is a huge job, even for a parent—let alone someone who might be a student, busy professional, recently married or young adult themselves. But the rewards and payoff are enormous—you can change a kid's entire life by spending positive time with them.

Cost: Free

Day #35

Let Them Have the Parking Space

-

Action: Yes, letting someone else have your hard-earned (and difficult to find) parking space might be a kindness that you think goes too far. But sit back and ponder for a moment: perhaps the other individual is having a bad day. Perhaps they need confirmation that the world is still good, still kind. Maybe they're late for the interview of their life, or they're hurrying to see an old friend who they've lost touch with for years.

So try it out. Sure, it's possible that they're not doing anything important—or they could just be changing the world. And that extra minute you give them by giving up your space might just change their life. Plus, they'll be amazed at your kindness and be reminded that the world isn't as selfish as they might've thought. They'll pay it forward.

If you're hesitant, try it on a day where you're not in a hurry, when you don't have anywhere to be. Spending your day off looking for parking might not be your idea of fun—but it could just give you some extra time to think. And you'll feel better, since you were kind to someone who you didn't even know.

Cost: Free

Day #36

Donate or Recycle Your Old Laptop & Electronics

-

Action: It's easy to toss your old monitor or laptop in the trash, dump it by the side of the curb without a second thought.

But that's not a very good idea, and it's not very kind—for either the planet, or those around you. So if you want to be kind to the world (and, as a by-product, yourself),

So head over to the EPA's website (epa.gov) to find a list of places in your area that will accept your old electronics for recycling. It might not seem like a big deal, but it is—all that plastic, metal and glass can be reused to make newer, faster and more awesome things in the future.

So if you want an iPhone 20 when it's released in fifteen years, be sure to take your current cell phone to a recycling center when you get that upgrade—don't just toss it in the trash!

Cost: Free

Day #37

Play Board Games with Senior Citizens at a Nursing Home

-

Action: It's easy to forget the elderly when our modern culture is so focused on the young. We can easily get caught up in our lives and the latest trends. This isn't a criticism, just a fact of modern life; with things moving so fast these days, it can be tough to remember that there are retired people out there who have become disconnected from life.

Which is probably why 60% of people living in a nursing home will never have a visitor.

These people were once just like you—working, going out with friends. But perhaps an ailment or the slow march of Father Time has forced them to move into a nursing or retirement home. These places can be difficult to visit, as it's hard to look at what fate is in store for us down the road. But ignoring these people isn't the solution! We can learn much from our elders by sitting down across from them and playing a simple board game—and the human interaction and conversation will do them a world of good. And, after the first visit, you might find yourself returning to learn more from these people who have lived rich and wonderful lives—in that way, they can repay your small kindness a hundred fold.

Cost: Free

Day #38

Help Your Elderly Neighbor. Take Out Their Trash, or Mow Their Lawn

-

Action: In the spirit of the previous day's kindness, today I want to invite you to help out your elderly neighbor with a little manual labor. As we all know, time has a way of slowing us all down. And it can make previously simple tasks like mowing the lawn or taking out the trash quite painful and difficult.

If you're a young (or younger) whippersnapper, however, you can use your good health and spry step to give them a little relief–and it doesn't cost you much more than a few minutes of your time. Now ,understand that not all elderly people will want or need your assistance; many enjoy these tasks, and it helps keep them sharp. But simply indicate to your elderly neighbors that the offer is there, and you are willing to help them with any manual activity that they can't quite do on their own any more.

By the same token, if you have a neighbor who has been recently injured, sick, or otherwise laid up, extend them the same kindness. They'll be thankful for the help, and even if they say no, they'll remember your generosity and concern in the future.

Cost: Free

Day #39

Wash a Stranger or a Friend's Car

-

Action: If your friend is obsessed with their car, you might want to ask permission before doing this—you don't want to scratch or apply the wrong wax to their baby! But if your friend or a stranger's car is looking in need of a good wash, this is a great way to surprise them and start (or end) their day with a big smile.

There's nothing quite like a shiny car, even if isn't all that new—so bust out the buckets, grab the hose and get to work (carefully!) making that car shine!

Cost: Free

Day #40

Play Cupid

-

Action: Love is difficult, even for the best of us. So when you have two friends or acquaintances that share some interests and seem perfect for each other, don't wait or keep quiet—make something happen and introduce them!

But don't make the common blind date mistake or the set-up. No one likes being set-up or blindsided. Instead, organize a get-together—a dinner, a small party, a night on the town—and invite both people along. Introduce them and casually mention their common interests/ground.

For example: "Betty Sue, you're from New Orleans, just like Tim Bob here!"

(I know you like my fictional names, don't you?)

Don't force things and don't be pushy—let things naturally unfold over the night. They just might be a match, and then, at their wedding (we're going full-on optimist here) you'll be able to tell everyone, "Told you so!"

Cost: Free

Day 41

Donate Your Stuff

-

Action: In a country like the United States, or other developed nations where we all have so much, it can be difficult to remember that a lot of people struggle without basic necessities.

Things we all take for granted like clothes or furniture. Our main problem is that we can't stop looking at our phone and all of our Twitter updates—some people don't even have a cell phone! Hey, don't worry; I do it, too. But maybe think about combing through that drawer of old phones and giving a couple of them away so that people in need can call a loved one. Or just have something nearby in case of an emergency.

So Instead of saving things in case you need them in 10 years, consider giving stuff to someone who needs it *now*. Here's a comprehensive list (bradaronson.com/where-to-donate/) of places where you can donate clothes, furniture, old phones, inkjet cartridges, children's clothes and books, appliances, electronics, cars, eyeglasses and more.

As an added bonus, you'll clear out some clutter and maybe even get a tax write-off while you perform this act of kindness. That's a win-win for everyone!

Cost: Free

Day #42

Send a Card to a Friend or Relative You Haven't Seen for Some Time

-

Action: We can sometimes get caught up with new things in our lives—making new friends, starting a new job, moving to a new place. During these times, we often forget about old friends and relatives we haven't seen in many months (or years). And, as we see them less and less, they become less prominent in our memories. It's a sad cycle—as we forget our old friends, we tend to forget and ignore them even more!

Don't let that happen; just because you haven't contacted someone in a while doesn't mean you can't do it right now. And don't wait for an excuse, like a birthday or other event to say hi. In fact, you can do it today, by just sending them a card. Ask them how their life is going, tell them a little about yours. It doesn't have to be a novel—just a simple note will do wonders to reestablish the connection that you once shared.

If you feel like a card is too much, or you don't have their address, an email or Facebook post will have much the same effect. But a handwritten card or letter, sent through the mail, can really be a nice touch to let someone know you haven't forgotten them.

For an added bonus, include a recent photo of yourself or your family.

Cost: Free

Day #43

Teach Someone Something

-

Action: Most of us are teachers and we just don't know it. We all have special skills that we can share with others, even if they aren't flashy, like playing the guitar like Jimi Hendrix. Maybe it's simply being kind to others and showing that you care (you have been following along, right?). Whatever your special talent is, you can teach and share your gift with others. Not only does this allow them to experience some of the same joy as you do from your knowledge, but you'll also learn something in the process.

Whatever your skill is, try to teach it to someone that can benefit–you might just change their life, no matter how small it seems on the surface.

Cost: Free

Day #44

Say "Yes" to Someone

-

Action: Rejection and failure are unfortunate facts of life; all of us experience them throughout our time here on planet Earth. Sometimes, however, the weight of all those people saying "no" can wear on our spirit and cause it to flag.

We've all experienced this—when it seems that nothing is working in our favor. Well, when things are going well for you, remember that there's someone out there struggling to just hear "yes" once.

And you can be that person. Who knows—maybe your "yes" can change the world. It did when Jack Thomas Andraka, then 15 years old, received a whopping 199 rejections for his request to do research at a variety of labs. One lab, however, had the foresight to say yes—and the teen used that yes to develop a test for pancreatic cancer that was over 100x more sensitive and 26,000x less expensive than existing tests.

That yes improved the world by an immeasurable amount.

Yours could do the same—so just say yes to someone that needs it!

Cost: Free

Day #45

Name a Star After Someone

-

Action: This act of kindness is extra cool because it lasts forever—what gift have you ever given that you can say that about? While cell phones and video game consoles break down and get replaced by the latest model, a star isn't going anywhere—it's always there, shining down from the night sky.

If you want to go the free route, you can look at a chart of the cosmos, and then find an appropriate star—there are millions out there to choose from, so pick one out that reflects your relationship with the person in question.

If you'd like to make the gift official, complete with a framed certificate, you can name a star after someone at Star Registry (starregistry.com)

Cost: Free (or around $55 if you use Star Registry)

CHEAP
(Easy)

Day 46 – Day 54

Day #46

Tape a few dollars in an envelope to a vending machine

-

Action: We've all been thirsty or hungry and passed by a vending machine. Only problem? We didn't have any small bills. Or no bills at all. And thus, we're forced to go onwards without getting a pick-me-up snack.

But hey, knowing this, you can help someone out in a similar predicament. Put a couple bucks in an envelope and tape it to the machine. The next person that comes along won't be able to thank you, but their stomachs certainly will—wherever you are.

Cost: $1 - $5

Day #47

Pay the toll for the driver behind

-

Action: Has someone ever done this for you? Probably not, which makes this random act of kindness all the more surprising and appreciated. We tend to be more frustrated than appreciate of the other drivers sharing the roadway with us.

But what if we could flip that around, and renew someone else's face in the goodness of other people. And maybe even get them to believe there are other good drivers out there (okay, maybe we shouldn't ask for too much).

When you pull up to the toll booth, instead of asking for your change, indicate to the attendant that the extra money you've given them is to cover the person behind you.

Cost: $1 - $10

Day #48

Put a coin in an expired meter

-

Action: Everyone hates getting tickets. It's a huge hassle—not only does it cost money, but you also have to mail it in. Sometimes you even have to visit the local office to get everything sorted out.

What if you could stop someone from getting one in less than two seconds?

Because that's how much time it takes to put another coin in their expired meter. Heck, you could put two in, and it would take you three seconds. You might think that no one would do this for you—and that's why no one does it!

So start a trend—if you pass by a meter that reads expired, don't let it sit there. Take action and help someone out. You'll make their day a whole better.

Cost: less than $1

Day #49

Leave your *New York Times* or *US Weekly* behind for someone else to read at the coffee shop, the doctor's office, or on a plane

-

Action: Nothing's worse than getting stuck somewhere with nothing to do. Staring at the wall isn't that much fun. That's why, whenever I'm in a public place where people have to wait, I'll leave behind my magazine or newspaper.

Don't litter—this doesn't mean you should leave your papers on park benches! But coffee shops, waiting rooms or planes/trains are all great places to leave your already read periodicals behind for someone else to enjoy.

Cost: $5 or less

Day #50

Be the person who puts a tip in the tip jar at the coffee shop

-

Action: Working at a coffee shop is a tough job. You're on your feet all day and dealing with customers who have complicated orders. But, unlike waiters, you don't usually get that many tips for all your hard work and dedication. That's a real bummer—these people put a lot of effort into your order and should be rewarded. Throw them a buck or two in the tip jar—it'll boost their morale.

You get extra points if you're the first person to put a tip in—science suggests that when other people see money in a tip jar, they're more likely to tip themselves.

And fewer people tip than you'd think, so they could really use that social nudge!

Cost: $1 - $2

Day #51

Say "yes" at the store when the cashier asks if you want to donate $1 to whichever cause

-

Action: Most of automatically say no to these types of requests without even listening to them. It's probably because every time we head to the store, the clerk offers to sell us a special membership program, a store card, or a warranty that we don't need.

But sometimes, they do have a worthwhile charitable cause to donate to. So listen closely, even if you don't want to, and next time a clerk asks you to donate a dollar on top of your order, do it!

This also works on some websites, where a retailer will ask you if you want to round up or donate a dollar or two for charity. Check the box and help someone in need out.

Cost: $1 or less

Day #52

Tape some change to a payphone with a card saying it is for whoever needs it

-

Action: Yes, a payphone—they still exist. Seriously! And when do you think people usually use them? Probably when their phone has died and they're in a serious bind. And, most likely they don't have change on them. Because, seriously, who thinks they'll ever have to use a payphone again...until they desperately need to use a payphone?

Which is why this is such a great, simple act of kindness—because you're probably bailing someone out who is having a really, really bad day. Maybe they're stranded a few miles from a gas station. Maybe their girlfriend left them on the side of the road. Or maybe they just need to hear a friendly voice.

Whatever the case is, help them out and leave them some change so that they can make that call.

Cost: less than $1

Day #53

Go into a book shop, and put a dollar between the pages of a self-help book, or one on finances

-

Action: This act of kindness is a fun, cool way to brighten someone's day. And it's just as simple as it sounds—all you need to do is head into a book store and put a dollar in the pages of a personal finance or self-help book. The next person who picks it up will probably be someone who could use it.

If you'd like, you can write a motivational message on the bill (this might be considered defacing the currency in your country...shhh, I won't tell on you). Something like *this is the first dollar of a million!* could be an inspiring message for someone who has struggled to make ends meet, or is having a rough time getting their life on the right track.

Even if the person's life is going okay, finding a buck is always a great moment—even better when you realize that some kind stranger left it behind on purpose.

Cost: $1

Day #54

Tape a dollar to the back of a candy bar in a gas station or convenience store with a note saying "Enjoy!"

-

Action: This kindness is along the same lines as Day 53's, except it has a sweet twist. It only takes a couple seconds—and will run you a dollar—but it's one of the cooler ways you can use a single buck to really spruce up someone's day.

The best part about this one is that the person won't even know about it until they pick it up. That's a great surprise!

Cost: $1

CHEAP (Medium)

Day 55 – Day 63

Day #55

Leave some extra quarters in the laundry room

-

Action: I think we can all agree that doing laundry and running out of quarters is just about *the worst...* especially when we run out of quarters for the dryer! No one likes sopping wet clothes, and this always seems to happen when the change machine is broken and there's no one else around to give us a helping hand.

So leave a couple of quarters on the washing machine, or on the table in the corner of the room. The next person who comes along will appreciate the generosity —and the clean clothes.

Cost: less than $1

Day #56

Bring a security guard a hot cup of coffee

-

Action: It's pretty easy to forget about security guards —they're usually pretty quiet, and go about their business with silent professionalism. But this is a tough job, since they have to remain vigilant and ready to act if anything on the premises goes wrong. And since their job is to watch for suspicious things, they can't just shuffle off for a coffee break whenever they want!

So bring the coffee to them. Not only will they appreciate the gesture, you'll be helping make the area safer by keeping the guard awake and on alert through the remaining hours of his shift.

Cost: $1 - $5

Day #57

Put a quarter in a row of candy machines for the kids to have!

-

Action: Do you remember begging your parents for a quarter to get some candy when you were little? I sure do...and while it's been a while since I've gotten candy from those little machines, cranking the metal knob until it spilled out, I don't think any of us quite forget that feeling.

There's something about turning that handle that's just so cool when you're a little kid. It's not even all about the candy (though the candy is pretty awesome!).

So help make a child's day and leave a quarter in the coin slot of the machines. Some lucky kid is going to be surprised at his good fortune and completely thrilled.

Cost: less than $1

Day #58

Drop a few coins in an area where children play, where they can easily find them

-

Action: This one is along the same lines as Day 57. When you're a kid, a couple quarters is a huge amount of money. It sounds funny to say that as an adult, but think back a little bit. I'm not even that old, and I remember being thrilled whenever I found a dime or quarter on the street. A dollar was like a million bucks!

So, if you're walking near a playground or park and have some change burning a hole in your pocket, drop it on the sidewalk. It might not make you rich, but the child who finds it will definitely feel that way!

Cost: $1 or less

Day #59

At the post office, leave some extra stamps at the stamp machine

-

Action: Nothing is worse than getting to the post office and realizing you've forgotten to stamp your letter. The line is long, and you only have your credit card—and the machine doesn't accept cash.

So imagine how awesome it would be if you found a couple stamps sitting there, waiting to be used? It'd save you a huge amount of time, and turn a negative experience into a profoundly positive one! Instead of being upset at the long line, you'd be ecstatic about a stranger's kindness.

So why don't you do this for someone else? Next time you buy stamps from the machine—or even from the cashier—leave a couple on the counter near the forms, or at the bottom of the machine. The next person coming along will probably do a double-take—hey, no one does this, sadly—but then a smile is sure to come across their face.

Cost: $1 - $2

Day #60

Next time you rent a "Redbox" movie, slip inside a dollar and a note saying "This movie's on us!"

-

Action: This one is cool for the next person who rents the movie. When you're done watching, put a dollar inside the case, underneath the DVD. The next person who happens to choose that movie from the Redbox machine will get an unexpected and cool surprise.

We all love free movies!

Cost: $1

Day #61

Tape a few dollars to the outside of a Redbox with a note saying "Enjoy some popcorn with your movie!"

-

Action: We're going full-on with the Redbox ideas for these couple of days...what can I say—I really enjoy movies (who doesn't). And, like most people, I enjoy eating some popcorn while I watch a good flick. The only thing better than popcorn, though, is...free popcorn.

Which is why you should tape a few dollars to the outside of the Redbox kiosk—or just tape a sealed package of popcorn instead!

Cost: $1 - $3

Day #62

Ask the grocery clerk to apply your unused coupons to another customer's items

-

Action: This one is a little unusual; everyone's first instinct, when they don't use a coupon, is to save it for later. But most of these coupons expire before we get the chance to come back to the grocery store.

So why not let someone else benefit? You get to do a good deed, and someone else gets to save some money. It's a win-win, and the coupon doesn't go to waste.

Plus, you don't have to remember to bring it with you next time you head out to the store.

Cost: $1 - $5 value (technically free, though)

Day #63

Buy a lemonade from a kid's lemonade stand

-

Action: Ah, the lemonade stand. Perhaps some of you remember setting up one of your own. Maybe even a couple of you managed to make a few dollars to buy something you wanted.

Support a child's entrepreneurial vision and buy a cup of lemonade when you see a stand in the neighborhood. Similarly, when kids have bake sales or group car washes, support these endeavors. It's only a dollar or two to you, but to kids, that's a lot of money!

Cost: $1 - $5

CHEAP
(Hard)

Day 64 – Day 72

Day #64

Pick someone out of the phonebook at random and send them a “Just Because” card

-

Action: This one is simple and is truly a random act of kindness. That’s what makes it stand out, though. Go through the phonebook, pick a person out, and send them a just because card. It’s easy for you, but it might just revitalize their spirit and remind them that the world is made up of good people.

They can't even ask you why you did it ;)

Cost: $1 - $5

Day #65

Frame your friend's favorite lyric or quote and give it to them with a nice note

-

Action: This one is not only a nice keepsake for the wall or desk, but it also shows that you've been listening and paying attention to your friend. Nothing is quite as personal as a favorite song or quote. These things usually have a great connection to the personal struggles and triumphs within our own lives.

When we recognize a friend's favorite song or quote, and then frame it, this act shows that we truly know who they are—and that we care about their life's story.

More than that, it shows we've listened to their problems, hopes and dreams—and that, no matter what, they don't have to face any of them alone.

Cost: $1 - $5 (more if you don't have a suitable frame)

Day #66

Buy a copy of your favorite book and donate it to your local library or hospital

-

Action: Have a book that changed your life or inspired you to do something great? You might think that no one else cares, or would want to read it.

You'd be wrong—if you thought it was great, then other people will probably love it, too. Don't keep wonderful things to yourself—allow others to benefit from your discoveries as well.

Better yet, donate copies of this book to your local library or hospital, for those who might not be able to afford it on their own—or for those who need to a good read to keep them occupied during a tough time.

Cost: $1 - $20 (most books can be bought used for less than $5, however)

Day #67

Contribute a small sum of money to grant a wish of a foster youth

-

Action: One Simple Wish (onesimplewish.org/grant-a-wish/) is an online directory of requests submitted by foster youth case workers. While simple and inexpensive by most standards—money for dance lessons, prom, or to be on the cheerleading squad—fulfilling these wishes can change a child's life.

Remember in previous days, when I suggested to put quarters in candy machines, or drop coins for children to pick up? Imagine that, for a few dollars, you could change more than the outcome of their immediate day. Imagine that you could change the outcome of a child's life by taking the time to donate a few dollars in support of their dreams.

Growing up in foster care is difficult, even with a caring foster family. Remind these children that the world cares, and that there's someone out there looking to help them out. They could really use it!

Cost: Varies (check the website)

Day #68

Carry around a $5 gift card so you can give it to someone who does something awesome. Or, create and carry "thanks for making my day" cards that you can give to people

-

Action: Hey, I know some of these ideas are pretty unusual. You might think that some of them are crazy—most of us give out gift cards on birthdays or holidays. But just for doing something cool on a regular day?

Yes—you should do it.

Giving someone a gift when it's expected is kind—but giving them when they don't expect it, and you don't have to (let's face it, not giving your best friend a present on her birthday probably isn't going to fly) is extra kind.

And it'll only cost you $5! If you don't have extra money, then you can just carry around "thanks for making my day" cards instead. People will appreciate the acknowledgment. They might even like it more than being paid—sometimes recognition is cherished way more than money!

Cost: $5

Day #69

Buy dessert for someone eating out alone

-

Action: You have to be careful with this one, since you don't want to make what might be a sad night out worse. But if you approach it the right way, buying someone something sweet—and showing them that they're not alone in the world—can be a great, kind touch.

Depending on the restaurant, you can either flag down your waiter or take the dessert over yourself. Either way, share a little ice cream (or pie—yum) with someone who might just need it!

Cost: $5 or less

Day #70

Give a lottery ticket to a stranger

-

Action: It may sound strange, but honestly why not? If they lose, then they have lost nothing, but have gotten the adrenaline rush of getting the "chance" to win something. However if they win, then you have made their day! Plus you have now given far more money than you spent on the ticket!

Now you can choose whatever style of ticket you want, but I would recommend something with low risk low reward. Or, in other words, a ticket that has a fairly high probability of winning, but the winnings might only be $5-$100 bucks. This, at least for me, would be far more exciting than a "big ticket lottery" because I knew I actually have a resonable chance of winning something!

Definitely something to try out :)

Cost: $1 - $5

Day #71

Shower the pediatric wing of a hospital with $1 coloring books and $2 boxes of new crayons

-

Action: Being a kid in the hospital is no small challenge. We all get scared and cranky when we're laid up and sick. The hospital is no fun, no matter how old you are.

So give kids a little bit of sunshine and hope, and donate coloring books and crayons to the pediatric wing of the local hospital. Better yet, bring them to the hospital and spend some time with the children, helping them draw and taking their mind off their current ailments. It might seem like a small thing for you, but happiness and positivity can help people heal. And knowing that there's good out there in the world never hurts, either, especially when you're small and the world seems scary and unfair.

Cost: $1 - $5

Day #72

Buy some diapers and wipes, and leave them on a changing board in a public washroom

-

Action: Being a new mom is tough (I'm imagining here, since I'm obviously not a mom). And it's probably a whole lot tougher when you get into the changing room...only to find that you're out of diapers. And baby wipes.

Uh-oh.

That's where you come in: buy some diapers and wipes, and help a harried, busy mom clean up her child. Under-slept plus overworked and in a rush is a recipe for forgetfulness for the best of us. Leaving diapers and wipes on the changing board can be a lifeline for moms caught in a bind. We all know that being a mom is tough—but it's often tricky to figure out how to help them out, especially for non-parents. This is a simple way to do it—and you don't even have to change the kid yourself!

Cost: $1 - $20

PREMIUM

(Easy)

Day 73 – Day 78

Day #73

If you know someone who is having a hard time financially, pop a $5, $10 or $20 note in an envelope, disguise your writing or type the envelope, and post it to them

-

Action: Most people don't like handouts and are too proud to either ask for money or accept your offer to help. So don't make a difficult situation worse by destroying their ego and pride–give them a couple bucks on the sly, anonymously.

But during tough financial times, it can also feel like you're alone on island–which is why receiving a few bucks in the mail can be such a breath of fresh air. It shows that your friends are listening and respectful of your situation. And that, if things get worse, you have people to rely on.

So slip a few dollars into an envelope–don't put a return address, and don't put any identifying marks inside–and mail it off. The person might never know who it's from, but they'll appreciate that someone cared.

And the cash will be appreciated, too.

Cost: Varies

Day #74

When it's summer and hot, give out cold Gatorades to your mail carrier and garbage men. When it's freezing outside offer hot chocolate to crossing guards, police officers and others

-

Action: These fine people walk miles a day and have tough, underappreciated jobs. And they do them rain or shine, without most of us noticing. Of course, we'd notice if our garbage was rotting in the hot sun, or our mail didn't come (maybe that'd be a good thing with all those bills...hmm...).

So say thanks to those keeping our streets clean, our mail coming, and our cities safe. Give them a little pick me up when the weather's tough—a Gatorade or bottle of water when it's sweltering, a hot chocolate or coffee when snow covers the ground.

They'll appreciate your gesture, just as you appreciate all the little, unsung ways they make your life easier and better.

Cost: $1 - $20

Day #75

In the middle of December, contribute to Operation Santa Claus

-

Action: The holiday season is a truly wonderful timc of year. Decorations abound, and people seem to be more generous and in a more giving mood. Maybe it's all the days off at work and school (or the eggnog—just kidding!).

For some, however, the holidays are less than cheery. While other people give gifts and see relatives, Christmas serves as a reminder of all the things missing from their lives—the gifts they can't buy for the children, friends or relatives important to them.

So give those people a helping hand, and help fulfill a wish for someone who needs a little extra help giving a gift by contributing to Operation Santa Clause. Go to the Post Office, snag one of the letters to Santa, and fulfill a wish for someone who needs help buying gifts. You'll remind them of what makes the holidays so special—the spirit of giving.

Cost: Varies

Day #76

Create a "dress-up" box for kids. Whether it's at your house, or you donate it to charity

-

Action: Kids love playing make believe. I don't need to tell you that—we were all kids once, pretending we were super heroes or princesses on exotic adventures to save the world or evil. As we grow older, however, and playing games goes out of style (along with thwarting imaginary villains), we tend to forget the simple joys of pretending to be someone else.

So feed your kids'—or others, by donating to charity, if you don't have kids of your own—imaginations by creating a dress-up box of fun costumes and clothing they can use to enact their crazy ideas with. It doesn't have to be expensive or elaborate; you can find all sorts of whacky stuff at flea markets, yard sales and the local Salvation Army. Just make sure you put it in the washing machine before you add it to the bin. In fact, going bargain hunting is a way to get the truly unique stuff—you'll be amazed at the weird, cool things you find if you search a little bit. Heck, it might even inspire your own imagination.

Just make sure to stay out from underfoot while the

kids are racing around the house, protecting it from an alien menace.

Cost: Varies

Day #77

Give a 100% tip At Your Favourite restaurant

-

Action: Tips are a server's bread and butter—while they earn an hourly wage, it's quite low. In other words, they depend on your generosity to make a living—so help them out and reward excellent service with a similarly excellent tip.

If you do this at your favourite restaurant, you have the added bonus of receiving better service the next time you go out to eat—so it's a win-win (as you may have noticed, I like win-win situations quite a bit!). A 100% tip might seem extravagant—and don't reward subpar service—but it will make a server smile. Instead of complaining about the person who sent back their steak three times, they'll talk with their coworkers about the awesome person who gave them a crazy tip.

Cost: Varies

Day #78

If you see someone who just got a parking ticket, put a note with money behind it saying "This sucks! But I hope this will help cover it. Have a great day! :)"

-

Action: Yes, paying for someone else's ticket. I've certainly lost it, haven't I?

No way! That's what makes this act of kindness so awesome: this will truly stand out and make the person notice. They'll think *woah, if someone did this for me, what can I do to help someone else?* This type of kindness makes the world a way better place—it takes a negative event (getting a ticket sucks) and turns it into an insanely positive experience.

See, sometimes a little craziness is a good thing!

Cost: Varies

PREMIUM
(Medium)

Day 79 – Day 84

Day #79

Bring doughnuts (or a healthy treat, like cut-up fruit) to work

-

Action: Everyone likes snacks, but no one has time on the rushed commute to work. Wake up, shower, shave, get the kids ready, get the car started, get gas—by the time they're near the office, most people are flooring it just to get in the parking lot before nine! With everything to do, there's no time to get breakfast or even really to think about it.

So wake up a little earlier—five minutes should do it—and stop by a local shop to pick up snacks for the office every once in awhile. Yes, sleeping is nice, but the energy from your coworkers will pick you up—the food will act as a morale booster and source of community. Pretty soon, everyone will be chipping in—they might bring in food, but they'll take out the trash, get your reports done faster, and make the workplace a much happier and more positivc place.

All for a couple of donuts or pieces of fruit. Not bad, right?

Cost: Varies

Day #80

Send dessert to another table

-

Action: This is a cool gesture, since everyone likes sweets (seriously, I think it's in our genes or something). Great candidates for your dessert are a couple madly in love, a family get-together, or a group of old friends catching up. Obviously you don't want to interrupt anything, so take stock of the situation to see if it's appropriate.

And if you've got money to spare, maybe buy dessert for everyone in the restaurant (okay, most of us will never do that–so stick with one table every once in awhile).

Maybe you'll start a trend and someone will buy *you* dessert down the line. Even if they don't, you'll make a table's evening for a night, and remind them of the kindness of random strangers.

Cost: $5 - $15

Day #81

Purchase some extra dog or cat food and drop it off at an animal shelter

-

Action: It's sad to think about, but some of our four legged friends go to sleep hungry—even after they've been rescued. Make sure this doesn't happen and buy some extra pet food to drop off at your local animal shelter. Fido and Garfield will thank you, even if they can't put it into words.

And the staff will be appreciative, since it gives their tight budgets just a little bit of relief.

Cost: $10 - $25

Day #82

Take all your change to Coinstar and donate your collection to charity

-

Action: If you're anything like me, you save your change in a big jar for a few months and then cash it in at the bank or local coin-counting machine. This is pretty fun—getting what seems like free money is always enjoyable!

But isn't the most fun just seeing how much you have in the jar (and placing friendly bets on the final tally with your friends)? I think the whole process would be even more enjoyable if we had a clear destination for that cash—a charitable one. I know, blowing it on a pizza party or new video game seems better in the short term, but the long term effect of your donation—both on yourself and others—will be hard to match by anything else the money could buy.

So put that "found" money to good work and donate it all to charity.

And maybe tell me how was in the jar. I'm curious!

Cost: Varies

Day #83

Carry around a care package of food or toiletries that you can give to a homeless person

-

Action: It's easy to ignore homeless people as we go about our day. But these people have had life knock them down—and many of them need a little helping hand to pick themselves back up. That can start with just maintaining a clean appearance and getting a little food in their stomach—basic human dignities that most of us take for granted.

So help these people back on their feet by giving them food or some basic toiletries. It might seem like a small step, but it could be a huge one in their lives.

Cost: $5 - $20

Day #84

Instead of asking Santa for something, bring him a Starbucks gift card!

-

Action: The Santa at the mall is probably more used to getting asked for things: new bicycles, baseball cards, video games. And, after seeing all those little kids and their overeager parents over a long day, what he could use the most is a nice, hot coffee.

So give him a Starbucks gift card as a thank you for sharing the Christmas spirit with hundreds of children. Share some Christmas spirit with him—the look on his face will be well worth it. He'll definitely be really surprised!

Cost: Varies

PREMIUM
(Hard)

Day 85 – Day 90

Day #85

Next time a homeless person asks you for change, buy them a meal

-

Action: Most of the time, someone begging for change sees their requests fall on deaf ears. Some of us are cynical, and think that they'll spend whatever we give them on drugs or alcohol; others of us are simply busy and in a rush.

However, just because these people are homeless doesn't mean they aren't human any more—which seems easy to forget, since they're disconnected from the world, isolated by their current situation.

So instead of giving him a few bucks, or worse yet ignoring a person, walk them over to a McDonald's or Subway and buy them a meal. That way, you make sure that your money goes towards food (if you're skeptical). And they get to eat a warm meal, something they might not have had for quite some time.

If you are feeling extremely generous, eat the meal with them and get to know them as well. This might be the greatest gift of all: actually talking and listening to them and their life story. Since so many people ignore them—or assume that their homelessness is a result of a catastrophic mistake of their own doing—this conversation could be the greatest kindness you can pay them.

We all want to be heard, and we all want to be noticed. So just sit and listen and take an interest in their life—you might just be surprised at what you learn!

Cost: $5 - $15

Day #86

Plant a Tree

-

Action: It's time to break a sweat and get your hands dirty. Yeah, that's right—we're going to plant an entire tree.

You can acquire saplings at your neighborhood nursery, or you can look for clean-up events and community gardens in the area. Either way, be prepared to grit your teeth, steel your back and get ready to feel tired. But in a good way—because you'll be helping the environment, making the neighborhood look better and pitching into a community effort.

Cost: Varies

Day #87

Offer to pay for someone's gas at a gas station

-

Action: Going to the pump is pretty dang tough these days, with gas prices at a premium. Paying for your own gas is probably painful enough—but paying for a stranger's might seem, well, like too much. After all, gas seems like it's more valuable than gold!

That's why you should offer to pay for someone's gas, though—because of its value and because everyone just hates paying for it. Everyone needs it though, so lighten the burden of a strange. Maybe a mom with a car full of kids, or a guy who looks like he's scrounging the quarters from his seat cushions.

Offer to pay and you'll make their day—and get them to where they need to go.

Cost: Varies

Day #88

Drop off a teddy bear at the police department to give to traumatized children

-

Action: Some children go through a lot. Growing up has a lot of challenges as it, without some traumatic event occurring to throw a wrench in our childhood. But you can provide a little bit of comfort for these kids by donating teddy bears to your local police department. It's a small gesture, but when it seems that the world is unfair and cold, the warmth of a simple teddy bear can remind them that there are kind, good things that happen, too.

And it gives them a friend to talk to and snuggle with when things are getting tough.

Cost: about $25

Day #89

Send _____ to your local volunteer firemen

-

Action: The best part about this kindness is YOU get to fill in the blank. Firefighters have one of the most important, but dangerous jobs out there. Every day they risk their lives to keep us and our families safe from harm. Their willingness to sacrifice their bodies and sometimes even their lives for others is truly commendable.

What's even more amazing is that some people volunteer for this job. That means they spend their off hours fighting fires—and they do it for free!

So think of a way that you can give back to these brave people. They're keeping your town safe—make their job a little easier and show that you've noticed their sacrifice.

Cost: Varies

Day #90

Take flowers to a hospital ward and give them to someone who hasn't had any visitors

-

Action: I don't think anyone likes being in the hospital. Aside from being sick or injured, it can be tough to be confined in a place that reminds us of our own mortality. Most of us are lucky enough to have friends and family visit us. In trying times, that support can really help our spirits—and it might well be the reason we make a full recovery.

So, when you're visiting a friend, colleague or relative, and notice someone who hasn't had any visitors, bring them flowers. Show them that someone out there is watching and paying attention to them. Prove to them that their life matters, and that you care.

You might just save their life.

Even if you don't, you'll definitely make their day.

Cost: $10 - $25

Outside the Box

(BIG IDEAS!)

Day 91 – Day 100

Day #91

Sell Hot Chocolate on a chilly day for charity!

-

Action: This is always better to do with a group of friends, but you can do it by yourself as well. Simply go out to a public place on a cold day, and offer hot chocolate for a charitable donation (or for free) until you run out. If you charge, pick a charity of your choice and make sure the customers know it's for charity. Then donate all the proceeds after you are done! I have personally did this with a group of my friends back in 2006 when the Tsunami hit Thailand. Surprisingly we made over $500 in a few short hours! It was super rewarding, and honestly extremely fun! I am planning on doing it again in the near future!

Cost: $25 worth of hot chocolate ingredients :)

Day #92

Have a clean-up party on the beach or at a park

-

Action: Not only will this kindness allow you to spend the day the beach or park—always a win in my book—but you'll make it more enjoyable for future visitors, too. Unfortunately, some folks throw their trash on the ground and make a mess of these beautiful places.

And sometimes the mess can get out of control. Local municipal workers might get to it, but with strained budgets, the cleanliness of the park might not be their top priority. Or they might just have too much cleaning and not enough manpower.

So take matters into your own hands and organize a clean-up party with your friends, family or coworkers. Not only will it make a great bonding experience and fun outing, you'll also help keep the world beautiful. Future beachgoers might not know it was you who cleaned the beach, but they'll appreciate the pristine sand and nice view!

Cost: Varies (free if you have tools and are within walking distance)

Day #93

Sign up for Amazon Smile

-

Action: This one is actually free, but if you buy a lot of stuff on Amazon, it can make a huge difference. Just go to smile.amazon.com and enroll in the program. Then, use the Amazon Smile website (same link as above) to do all your shopping. Amazon will donate their own money—at no charge to you—when you purchase items. Yes, the same ones you normally buy—except Amazon will donate 0.5% of the purchase price to your charity of choice!

Cost: Free (and then spend on whatever goodies you normally buy)

Day #94

Play Music for the Bedridden People

-

Action: If you're a musician living in NYC, Philadelphia, Washington, DC, Nashville or Miami, you can volunteer through the nonprofit Musicians on Call (musiciansoncall.org) to deliver a live, in-room performance to patients undergoing treatment or unable to leave their beds. Add a dose of joy to life in a healthcare facility by bringing the healing power of music to people who need it.

Cost: Free (if you live in the area)

Day #95

Send a care package to a solider

-

Action: Don't forget about those who fight to keep us safe every day. Half a world away, soldiers are often out of sight and thus out of mind—but it doesn't have to be that way! Show that you appreciate their bravery, dedication and sacrifice, and send them a care package. Fill it with reminders of home, and things they might not be able to get overseas.

It'll remind them of what they're fighting for during the difficult times away from their families.

Cost: Varies

Day #96

Be an Organ Donor

-

Action: I understand that some people don't want to donate their organs because of religious or spiritual beliefs. I respect that! Many of us who aren't organ donors, however, don't sign up because we forget or we just don't check the box when we renew our license.

But we should—and it only takes five minutes. Head over to the official Organ Donor site (organdonor.gov) to find out how to become a donor in your state.

Then, when you die (we all do eventually), your organs can be used to save lives. One person's organs can save up to 8 lives. If you want to know more—or you're still not sold on the benefits—the Mayo Clinic has an excellent article answering frequently asked questions and concerns about organ donation.

Cost: Free

Day #97

When a girl has her "time of the month" put together a huge gift basket of goodies, encouragement, and fun!

-

Action: This one's for the ladies (or husbands, if you want to earn some points with your significant others). Look, "that time of the month" isn't all that fun—so make it a little easier, and show that you care about your friend by giving her a gift basket or having a fun night with her. Good ideas include renting her some sappy movies, or buying her ice cream and chocolate!

More than the gifts, it'll be nice for them just to know that someone was thinking and looking out for them enough to notice!

Cost: Varies

Day #98

Donate your old car, or any scrap metal, to a worthy charity!

-

Action: This is really a "win-win" for most people. Since there are numerous scrap metal charities that will take your scrap metal off your hands for free, and use the money they get for the metal for worthy causes.

This won't cost you dime, AND the proceeds go towards making the world a better place!

If you are in Canada (like me), a notable charity that does this is Scrap Cars Not Kids. They take old cars and scrap metal, and donate the proceeds towards ending the exploitation of children in sexual slavery. A HUGE issue in current society that is rarely talked about.

If you are in the U.S., you could try Car Donation Network. Or possibly find something local.

And finally, if you are in the UK, you can try Scrap 4

Charity.

This really pays homage to the old saying “One persons trash, is another persons treasure.”

Day #99

Wash cars all day for free with a group of friends!

-

Action: Organize a community car wash with your friends, and then wash everyone's car for free. Better yet, charge a few bucks, indicate that it's for a good local charity, and then give all the money away when all the soap suds and water has cleared at the end of the day.

People get a good wash for their car at a good price, a charity gets to benefit—what's not to like about this kindness? You'll even get some exercise—and maybe even a tan!

Cost: Varies

Day #100

If you're a business, leverage what you do every day to do good and perform acts of kindness

-

Action: I've mentioned this throughout the book, but it bears reiterating at the end. Our lives are busy; I know mine is, and I'd bet yours is pretty hectic, too. We all have responsibilities like school, jobs and friends that take up a lot of our focus.

Sometimes, though, the grind of daily life can blind us to some of the more important things in this world. Money isn't evil by any means—but we all know businesses who focus on the bottom line above all else.

That doesn't usually turn out so well—for the business owner, the community, or the customers who support it.

If you're a business owner, try to enhance the world and give back, instead taking. Always give more value than the money you receive (this is a good way to *stay* in business, anyway). And don't cut corners or ignore people's requests for help just because it might cost you a little time or money.

Do things the right way and the world will be better for it.

As an example, Plaza Cleaners in Portland, OR posted the above sign. In case you can't read it, the sign simply says, "If you are unemployed and need an outfit clean for an interview, we will clean it for free."

This probably doesn't cost them much—maybe a few bucks a week and few extra minutes. But in a country that's been wracked with unemployment since the 2008 recession, it means a lot to the community and those looking for work—even if they don't take the place up on its offer. Just knowing that there are people that *care* is often enough.

As another example, Rotation Records in Norristown,

PA heard about an 11-year old battling cancer whose dream is to be a singer. They offered her an opportunity to have a recording session and red carpet party at their studios, which was a huge hit.

Rotation Records used its expertise and knowledge to grant a little girl's dream. They'd probably thrown dozen of release parties and hosted hundreds of recording sessions—and so they were able to use all those unique skills and abilities to throw one extra special party and recording session.

And to the little girl, it probably meant everything.

So when you see an opportunity to use your skills, expertise and knowledge to help someone in need who's having a tough go of things, don't wait. Offer your assistance.

Because it's always nice to be reminded that the world is, at its core, a good, kind place—and it's our job to keep it that way.

Together!

Cost: Varies

CONCLUSION

Alright, that's it! That's everything. You know have MORE than enough idea's to get started in sharing the love in your neighbourhood. But here's what you should do first.

1. Leave an Amazon review

If you enjoyed this book, then please take a moment to leave a review on Amazon.

This truly means a lot to me, and is a perfect way of showing your gratitude if you felt this book helped you in any way.

2. Go out and try one, or ALL, or these Acts of Random Kindness for yourself!

Seriously, go out and try these for yourself! Even if you only do one. Or even if you only do the free and easy ones. All kindness is *good* kindness. So get out there and share it!

3. Join my Newsletter!

If you haven't already, sign up for my mailing list so you can be updated whenever I have a new book out!

You can do so at: www.100daysofadventures.com

In fact, email me at

AbeFalls@100daysofadventures.com, and email me

what YOU want my next book topic to be about!

Simply type in the subject line "100 days of... (Fill in the blank)", and then tell me WHY you think I should write about that topic. I always read these emails, and honestly they are my favourite part of my day. Interacting, and getting to know you guys is seriously the BEST part about this job!

Alright, that's it! Thank you so much again for downloading this book. I truly hope you enjoyed it.

Made in the USA
Columbia, SC
25 November 2017